Australian Wildlife from A to Z

Animal Kingdom ABCs

A Photo Journey Exploring the Fascinating Creatures of Australia with Fun Facts for Kids Who Love Wild Animals

by Michele Renee Acosta

Published by
Just Because...Books
an imprint of
My Extra Umbrella

Australian Wildlife from A to Z:
A Photo Journey Exploring the Fascinating Creatures of Australia
with Fun Facts for Kids Who Love Wild Animals
Copyright © 2025 by Michele Renee Acosta

Library of Congress Cataloging-in-Publication Data is available.
Library of Congress Control Number: 2024922755

ISBN (hardcover): 979-8-89615-062-6
ISBN (paperback): 979-8-89615-002-2
ISBN (ebook–Kindle edition): 979-8-89615-009-1
ISBN (ebook–EPUB edition): 979-8-89615-069-5

Published by
Just Because...Books
an imprint of My Extra Umbrella
1968 South Coast Highway
Suite 891
Laguna Beach, California 92651
Publisher@MyExtraUmbrella.com

This is Book 2 in the *Animal Kingdom ABCs* series.

Books in the *Animal Kingdom ABCs* series can be read in any order.

Printed in Laguna Beach, California, U.S.A.

First Edition

Author's Note

Welcome to *Australian Wildlife from A to Z*, a book that invites young children to embark on an exciting adventure through Australia's diverse wildlife. This book, part of the *Animal Kingdom ABCs* series, is designed to introduce children to wildlife from across the Australian continent in a way that's both fun and engaging. While it may look like a traditional ABC book, it goes far beyond teaching the alphabet. Instead, it's a window into the fascinating world of the animals and other wildlife that inhabit this unique part of the globe.

Each book in the series is organized alphabetically, which helps young pre-readers easily follow along and engage with the content. However, it's not about "learning the ABCs" in the usual sense. Rather, it's about sparking curiosity about wildlife and showing how vast and varied the animal kingdom can be, one letter at a time. Many of the wildlife names in this book—like *quokka* and *cassowary*—are not words typically found in a traditional ABC book. That's part of the fun! While these words may be challenging to pronounce, it's a great way for children to expand their vocabulary and learn about creatures they might never have encountered before. Note that no wildlife exists in Australia that begins with the letter X. Rather than exclude a letter from the alphabet, I've offered the opportunity for children to use what they've learned about wildlife from this part of the world to imagine an animal with features needed to survive in the habitats and climates on this continent.

Before reading for the first time, I encourage you to have a conversation about the animals children might expect to see in a book about Australian wildlife. Ask children to share what they already know about animals in general and Australian animals in particular. At the end of the book, you'll find fun facts about Australian wildlife, as well as critical-thinking questions designed to inspire deeper conversations. These questions are perfect for further exploration of the topic and for encouraging curiosity and a life-long love of learning.

Remember, the goal of this book is discovery and wonder. It's okay if the animal names are tricky—that's why I included helpful pronunciations and facts! This book, and the series as a whole, aims to offer children an opportunity to explore the natural world continent by continent, fostering a sense of adventure, awe, and connection to the animals with which we share this planet.

Thank you for joining me on this exciting adventure through Australia's animal kingdom!

Happy exploring!

Michele Renee Acosta

If you love *Australian Wildlife from A to Z*, explore the rest of the *Animal Kingdom ABCs* series. Each book features real animals, surprising facts, and fun ways to spark curiosity. You'll also find other fiction and nonfiction series for children ages 3–8, along with a little something extra to download and enjoy.

A

Australian Sea Lion

B

Bearded Dragon

C

Cassowary

D

Dingo

E

Echidna

F

Frilled-Neck Lizzard

G

Green Tree Frog

H

Helmeted Honeyeater

I

Inland Taipan

Jewel Spider

K

Kangaroo

L

Lorikeet

M

Mulga Snake

Numbat

O

Olive Python

Platypus

Q

Quokka

R

Redback Spider

S

Sugar Glider

T

Tasmanian Devil

U

Ulysses Butterfly

V

Variegated Fairywren

W

Wombat

What would your animal eat?

Where would your animal live?

X

Name
Your Animal!

X _____

Invent an animal that could live in Australia's Outback!

Y

Yellow-Footed Rock Wallaby

Z

Zebra Finch

Would You Believe?

Australian Sea Lions can dive over 980 feet deep to hunt squid and fish! That's the length of 24 school buses lined up in a row!

Bearded dragons "wave" an arm in slow circles! Scientists believe it's a form of communication.

Cassowaries have knife-like claws on each foot and can run up to 30 miles per hour.

Dingoes don't bark like regular dogs. They mostly howl and yelp to communicate.

Echidnas lay eggs even though they're mammals! They belong to a rare group called monotremes!

Frilled-Neck Lizards open a large, colorful "frill" around the neck when frightened.

Green Tree Frogs can stick to smooth surfaces with toe pads that act like suction cups.

Helmeted Honeyeaters have brush-tipped tongues for sipping sticky sap from eucalyptus trees.

Inland Taipans are the most venomous snakes in the world.

Jewel Spiders build orb-shaped webs and are known for their shiny, spiky bodies.

Kangaroos can't walk backward and use their strong tails for balance.

Lorikeets are known for their playful behavior. They also mate for life.

Mulga Snakes are really long—up to 11 feet. One bite has more venom than most other snakes!

Numbats eat up to 20,000 termites in a single day using their long sticky tongues.

Olive Pythons can grow over 13 feet long. They aren't venomous, but instead squeeze their prey.

Platypuses are one of only two mammals that lay eggs. (The other is the echidna.)

Quokkas look like they are smiling, so they are known as the world's "happiest" animals.

Redback Spiders are related to black widows. Females are larger and more venomous than males.

Sugar Gliders glide from tree to tree using stretchy skin between their front and back legs.

Tasmanian Devils are small but have one of the strongest bites for their size of any mammal.

Ulysses Butterflies use their blue wings to attract mates and warn predators.

Variegated Fairywrens change color during breeding season. Males grow bright blue feathers to impress the females!

Wombats have cube-shaped poop to mark their territory. It doesn't roll away!

Yellow-Footed Rock Wallabies can leap across steep rocks with ease thanks to grippy feet.

Zebra Finches learn to sing by copying their dads, but each bird's song ends up a little different.

What Do You Know?

Use these questions to spark curiosity and conversation. Talk about details you notice in the photos and what you've learned together from *Would You Believe?* facts and other sources.

1. Which Australian animal surprised you the most?
   What about that animal is most interesting to you?

2. Which animal do you think would be easiest to spot in the wild?
   Which animal do you think would be hardest to spot? Why?

3. Which Australian animal would you want to see up close? Why?

4. How might a strong tail help an animal in the wild?

5. Which two Australian animals lay eggs even though they are mammals?

6. How might sharp claws, long tails, or stretchy skin help an animal?

7. A marsupial is a kind of animal that carries and feeds its babies in a pouch on its belly. Kangaroos, sugar gliders, Tasmanian devils, wombats, quokkas, numbats, and yellow-footed rock wallabies are all marsupials. How do you think these pouches help marsupial babies survive in the wild?

8. What do you think animals that live in deserts might have in common?

9. Which Australian animals do you think live in groups? Which ones might live alone?
   What clues helped you decide?

10. Pick an Australian animal. How do you think this animal protects itself from danger?

11. If you made up a new Australian animal, where would it live and what would it eat?

12. If you could be one Australian animal for a day, which animal would you choose? Why?

How Do You Say It?

Australian Sea Lion
(aw-STRAYL-yuhn SEE LY-uhn)

Bearded Dragon (BEER-did DRAG-uhn)

Cassowary (KAS-uh-wair-ee)

Dingo (DIN-goh)

Echidna (ih-KID-nuh)

Frilled-Neck Lizard (FRILD-nek LIZ-urd)

Green Tree Frog (GREEN TREE FROG)

Helmeted Honeyeater
(HEL-mit-id HUN-ee-ee-ter)

Inland Taipan (IN-luhnd TIE-pan)

Jewel Spider (JOOL SPY-der)

Kangaroo (KANG-uh-ROO)

Lorikeet (LOR-uh-keet)

Mulga Snake (MUL-guh SNAKE)

Numbat (NUM-bat)

Olive Python (OL-iv PY-thon)

Platypus (PLAT-uh-puhs)

Quokka (KWOK-uh)

Redback Spider (RED-bak SPY-der)

Sugar Glider (SHOO-gur GLY-der)

Tasmanian Devil (taz-MAY-nee-uhn DEV-uhl)

Ulysses Butterfly (yoo-LISS-eez BUT-er-fly)

Variegated Fairywren
(VAIR-ee-uh-gay-tid FAIR-ee-ren)

Wombat (WOM-bat)

Yellow-Footed Rock Wallaby
(YEL-oh-foot-id ROK WOL-uh-bee)

Zebra Finch (ZEE-bruh FINCH)

Sources Australian Geographic: Wildlife and Conservation (https://www.australiangeographic.com.au); Australian Museum: Animal factsheets (https://australian.museum); Australian Reptile Park (https://reptilepark.com.au); Australian Wildlife Conservancy: Species Conservation (https://www.australianwildlife.org); Australia Zoo (https://australiazoo.com.au); BBC Earth (https://www.bbcearth.com); Birdlife Australia: Species profiles (https://birdlife.org.au); Butterfly House: Australian butterfly species (https://www.butterflyhouse.com.au); National Geographic Kids: National Geographic Partners (https://kids.nationalgeographic.com/animals); San Diego Zoo Kids: San Diego Zoo Wildlife Alliance (https://kids.sandiegozoo.org); World Wildlife Fund: Australian species(https://www.worldwildlife.org)

More animals.
More fun.
More to explore.